TW

20 POEMS, 20 MENTAL DISORDERS, MANY INTERPRETATIONS

Sonia Clemente

Presentation by *BookLeaf Publishing*

Web: www.bookleafpub.com

E-mail: info@bookleafpub.com

ISBN: 9789358360035

First edition 2021

I would like to thank my friends for giving me the inspiration I needed to write these poems. To anyone going through any of these mental disorders, remember, you are never alone no matter how isolated you feel.

DID

Who am I?

I have people surrounding me, I can feel THEM staring at me...

fighting to take control over the body I live in.

What is wrong with me?

Why does everyone run away when THEY show up,

I can feel the fire burn inside of me every time I think about THEM taking control,

Why can't they leave me alone? What did I do wrong?

I didn't ask to be born with THEM,

I never asked to be so brutally taken control of!

The strong apprehension,

I don't know what comes next and it scares me...

Does anyone understand me?

Why don't they know?!

It frustrates me to the bitter end,

Sometimes the darkness starts to engulf me and my eyesight is blotched,

I look through my eyes but it's not me who is seeing...

I'm looking at a TV screen inside my head that only occasionally I feel I'm in.

It's hard finding someone who will be willing to be-friend not just me but them...

Sometimes they are my only companion,

Maybe they will always be my only companion...

SOCIAL ANXIETY

I'm panicking,

I don't know where I'm at,

I don't know what is happening.

My heart is speeding up...

The blood in my ears is pounding,

I'm sweating profusely...

There are too many people around,

I need to get out,

I need to escape,

Can everybody please quiet down I'm trying to think!

With all of these thoughts rushing into my brain I can't help but overthink!

I'm scaring myself even more than I should but I can't help it...

I never could.

I always drown in my own darkness when I'm surrounded by people...

They call me anti-social,

They call me an outcast,

I don't choose to be both,

I'm just labeled without consent.

I have no clue what I'm doing...

I try to go back to the present but I'm still stuck inside my mind,

I think I need help but I'm too afraid to ask for it.

When I finally do come back to my senses I feel everyone staring at me

Stop looking at me!

I run away...

PTSD

I've done it again,

I scared the people who tried to help me

I scared the person who tried to touch me

I HURT them....

I can't help it,

I try to stop but before I know it I'm flinching...

I'm flinching from fear that's been embedded in me for a long time,

I flinch because I don't know if they will hurt me,

I flinch because I'm taken back to the memories that dictated who I am today...

Everyday is a nightmare,

I feel on edge...

Every hand or movement that catches my eye is my enemy,

Every hand is the the shadow of a memory,

Every hand is dangerous...

What will come next?

A punch?

A slap?

Or the feeling of being touched not being able to say no?

I would much rather live inside my walls,

No one comes near,

No one has the opportunity to hurt me...

I've already forgotten the last time I was held and felt safe,

I forgot the comfort I found in being with the people I deemed safe.

I know that they won't hurt me,

I know they are only trying to help me,

I know they are people I can trust,

Yet even to them I flinch away,

My own friends...

My own family...

Sometimes I want to numb myself,

Forget that this paranoia is inside me,

Forget I ever felt UNSAFE...

I know I can't do that,

I know I never will...

I yearn for affection I'm scared to receive.

BULIMIA

I'm hungry again.

I'm always hungry these days.

The food I eat can't stay down,

and if I do somehow manage to swallow,

my appetite goes into a frenzy...

Sometimes food is what controls me,

Sometimes just looking at it is enough for me.

Tip top shape I say as I miss breakfast,

Tip top shape I say as I exercise till I can barely walk.

Everyone compliments me when I do this,

Such a great figure! They say

You must live such a healthy life! They say

If only they knew what went on behind the scenes...

If I eat more than I think I should,

I shame myself...

Why would you do that?

Don't you know it's not good to be like this?

These are the thoughts that cloud my mind as I proceed to purge.

When my barrier breaks and I don't follow my own strict rules,

The dam that held back my hunger breaks down...

The cloud of plausibilities clouds my judgement and I eat more than I should.

I eat and I eat, and when I finally notice...

I'm filled with instant regret.

I fill my life up with even stricter rules to make up for the days I don't stop myself...

It's hard staying the perfect image I imagine myself to be...

It's hard living with the person staring back at me from the mirror...

It's hard imagining the person people see.

NPD

Why are people like this?

Why can't they accept that I am the main character?

Isn't it obvious?

Vulnerability isn't in my vocabulary,

To be the best I always wish to be,

I look down on those who belong under my feet,

I never let them get a step ahead of me.

I can bend people to my will-

Trust me, I know best.

I can NEVER lose,

I'm ALWAYS right,

I was raised to be an Emperor,

Call me your highness because you will soon bow at my feet.

Give me your praise,

I'm the lead role in this movie after all,

Give me this,

Give me that,

I'm your commander and your my army...

Feel lucky to fight for royalty.

Never go against me unless you want to face the wrath of my anger,

I deserve everything I've ever had,

But you never will.

ADHD

Tap tap tap,

There I go again,

Click click click,

Why can't I stay still?

I look around,

It's too quiet,

I need to move,

How is everyone still?

I feel uncomfortable,

I can't pay attention,

It's hard.

I should've taken my meds but I hate how slow I get...

I don't wanna feel fuzzy again.

I start moving my leg unconsciously,

Up and down up and down it goes,

I can't stop it, it's hard to...

I try to concentrate but that just makes things worse.

What am I having for dinner today?

What will I do when I get home?

Did I remember to make my bed this morning?

Did- Oh! What's that?

A constant buzzing at the back of my head my head,

I can't control them,

It's frustrating,

What's wrong with me?

I'm always either at a high or low,

Never in between,

No one understands,

I wish someone did...

BURNOUT

I work and I work,

Full of energy,

I'm ready,

I'm ready to blaze through my work.

Tap tap tap,

I'm almost done,

Tap tap tap,

I should start this project too,

Tap tap tap,

My parents come in with my report card,

Tap tap tap....

5 more assignments left.

Tap tap- I stop tapping,

I can't bring myself to continue...

I feel exhausted,

I feel hungry,

I can't get off my chair,

I feel sluggish,

I feel tired…

Time is slowed down,

I turn slush,

I'm overheated,

I pushed myself too far again…

Ding! A notification appears on my phone.

"Hey wanna hang out today?"

I start to feel frustrated,

Why can't they leave me alone!

I just want to be alone…

I need to finish,

I need to do what I need to do,

I can't slack,

Yet I stayed glued to my chair...

I'll finish it tomorrow,

I'll finish it tomorrow,

Tomorrow tomorrow tomorrow,

I always say tomorrow,

but tomorrow never comes.

DRUG ADDICTION

I'm crazed,

I can't stop.

Every time I try- I find myself being hypnotized,

Swooning back and forth,

They are my only comfort,

They are my lover,

They gift me life...

I feel like I'm on top of the world,

The ruler of my own kingdom,

I finally got my reins back...

No one can stop me,

I keep doing what I do to achieve my satisfaction.

You can't tell me to just step away!

it's not easy....

They feel like family,

People don't abandon family.

I find it ironic.

I think that,

yet I keep myself isolated for little ziplock bags,

These are the only friends I'll ever need.

Even if it's for a few fleeting hours,

I will be happy,

Anything for happiness I say,

Anything to numb the pain away...

I try to cut the the binding ropes,

But every time I manage to break away,

I stumble and fall into the same old cycle,

Over and over and over again with no end.

Dirty used needles,

Rolled up blunts,

Cut up straws,

I'm tired of this...

I don't remember how it happened,

Was it the urge to fit in?

Was it the need to be numb?

Did I ever regret what I did?

I don't remember.

SCHIZOPHRENIA

Hey who's that over there?

The tall man with a funny hat,

He follows me around all day.

I've tried talking to him before,

But he won't say a thing,

He just copies everything I dare to do.

Sometimes when I'm lying in bed,

The shadow man comes to mess with my head,

He feeds me poison each night,

And I drink without a fight.

I see things people don't see,

The monsters that never let me be,

Never a chance of peace,

A river of shadows always following me,

Tried to escape,

but all they do is tie me down with heavier chains.

Sometimes I even get stuck inside my head,

I don't mean too...

But I'm taken into a different reality.

It's hard living a life no one else can see,

But what else can I do?

I live in a nightmare only I can see.

BIPOLAR

What are we up to today?

Should we go skiing?

Should we go to the park?

Should I finish all of the projects that need to get done?

I pass many sleepless nights but I'm happy as can be,

I'm mostly full of energy and feel like I can take things head on,

But sometimes I start to get low,

I start to feel drowsy,

My sleepless nights start to catch up to me.

I run out of fuel and my depression comes back like a boomerang,

It comes and goes when it pleases,

It never gives me a warning.

One thought after another runs through my head...

Am I good enough?

Am I too quiet?

What do people think of me?

All of this passes in a wave,

I'm back to being the other part of me,

I'm glad to be me again,

I'm glad to be able to do the things I always want to do.

I swing back and forth between day and night,

Between sleepless nights and daily naps,

Never being able to keep both feet on the ground.

I'm a dysfunctional motor,

I come on and off...

Sometimes at the most inconvenient situations.

I wish to be at peace...

but I know I'll never be,

So I'll just keep on smiling as my world falls apart.

OCD

Everything must be perfect,

This goes there and that goes there,

Everything is in order,

nothing out of place...

I'm calm.

But the moment something is moved out of place,

My world shatters.

It bothers me like a bug,

A constant buzzing by my ear that doesn't seem to go away till it's fixed.

7 steps to the bathroom,

1 minute to brush my teeth,

30 minutes to take a bath,

10 minutes to get ready,

At 6:00 on the dot I head out the door,

My left foot then my right.

Everything must go as planned.

If I mess up my steps I need to start again.

There must be no inconvenience,

Everything should go as planned.

My notes must be color coded,

My notebooks must be in order,

It takes time but at least I'm satisfied.

When I come home I must change,

What is worn outside can't be worn inside,

I came into contact with many things,

I need to wash my hands,

I scrub and I scrub and I scrub-

My hands still feel dirty.

I need to keep scrubbing.

30 minutes later and I feel clean enough.

My bed sheets must be laid down like this,

I can't sleep if it's not,

I need to fall asleep at exactly 10pm,

No exceptions.

I repeat this routine every single day.

I've memorized it so that it is perfection.

Nothing's out of place.

I'm calm.

I'll always be calm if I follow these simple steps.

ALICE IN WONDERLAND SYNDROME

I come back to bed half asleep,

In and out of sleep I come and go when I notice something,

My walls are small,

With a lift of a hand I can reach the ceiling,

I'm in a funhouse with peculiar mirrors,

I turn into a giant at night...

This doesn't scare me,

I think it's pretty cool,

I'm in a fairytale where giants exist,

Nothing bad is happening,

Everything just looks funny.

I've tried explaining it but no one seems to really understand,

As I grow older these nightly visions become rare,

Slowly they fade,

Slowly they disappear.

Till one night I find myself back inside the wacky mirrors,

But this time it's different,

I'm not a giant,

I'm an ant stuck in a big bed.

I wasn't scared before,

Im still not scared now.

Small like a toy soldier,

Or big like a giant,

I wonder what it will be like tomorrow night.

DYSLEXIA

It's hard to write words when they look like scribbles,

It's hard to read when everything looks like an unsolvable puzzle.

Ever since I was a kid words have been muddled,

I was called a genius till I had to write on paper,

Scribble after scribble,

I just couldn't get it right.

Words were blurred over by an invisible hand,

I was blind to something people said I desperately needed.

I wasn't like others.

I learned to say a few words when I was two,

It was hard learning the language I was born into.

I was called stupid and disobedient,

"You do this on purpose"

I never did,

I never knew how to fake getting something right.

I never knew how to make things easier,

Words always swirled around me...

Confusing me till the bitter end.

It felt hopeless,

Sometimes it still does

.

STOCKHOLM SYNDROME

They are my kidnapper,

They keep me alive,

They keep me fed and clothed.

All I have to do in return,

Is love them .

To outsiders it may look weird,

But I think it's fine,

They repaid me with kindness,

So I will repay the favor.

I know they are a kind soul,

They must be,

Even if they kidnapped me,

I know they won't hurt me.

I'm tied to them...

I owe them the life they allowed me to live.

INSOMNIA

I can't sleep,

Every time I try,

An invisible hand pries my eyes open.

Don't sleep,Don't sleep,Don't sleep,

A silent voice whispers in my ear while I'm internally screaming for it to go away...

My eyes are burning,

I'm feeling lightheaded.

I beg it to leave me alone...

I have a killer headache that just won't go away.

Sometimes I feel like a fox,

Always up at night,

Always sleeping the day away.

There are many things I wish to do,

These sleepless nights chip away at the life I try to live.

Slowly I start to numb,

Passing the day like a movie clip in a montage I'm not in.

It's hard focusing on what's in front of me.

Little dark bags of stress start to appear under my eyes,

Slowly I start to succumb into this seemingly endless cycle,

The chapters of my life start to pass like a breeze.

Whenever I manage to get some sleep,

An internal timer starts ticking away,

Tick tock goes the clock,

Ring Ring Ring,

Wake up.

ASPERGERS

I'm surrounded by sharks,

They are the barriers that keep me in my little island,

I remain alone with only few to talk to.

I like to think that I rolled a dice,

A dice that dictated my life.

I rolled it and got the lottery...

At least according to those around me.

I may be intelligent,

But it's hard being alone.

No one seems to really understand me,

I'm always in my own little world.

Some tell me I'm difficult...

Emotionless,

But what they don't understand is that it goes both ways.

I spectate my own life as others walk by...

I'm a ghost,

Just floating from place to place,

Always physically present,

But never quite there.

I love to be alone,

I love to have these thoughts running through my mind.

No one to tell me I'm not human...

But sometimes,

Sometimes it gets lonely.

After a while the lack of companionship takes a toll,

After a while it starts to hurt.

I don't have a disease,

At least I like to think I don't.

I know that I cannot be cured,

I know that some things can lessen my burden...

I'm not sick,

I'm just a little different.

I may be born with a slight advantage,

But if you look at the bigger picture...

Who really has the short end of the stick, you or me?

TOURETTE SYNDROME

I can't control myself,

I twist and turn,

I say random words.

Every time I try to hold back,

It gets worse.

What I have is like repellent,

It keeps everyone away from me.

Sometimes it gets physical,

I punch and I kick,

No real target,

just movement.

I scream and shout,

I try not to bounce about.

School isn't easy,

Insult after insult comes my way,

I'm an attention seeker and a copycat.

I'm out of control,

I'm even obnoxious to some.

I deal with agoraphobia in my daily life,

But slowly comes a friend here and there,

Slowly I ease my way back on the road I call life,

Slowly I learn to accept this part of me.

BODY DYSMORPHIA

The mirror never lies,

At least that's what I say.

Everyday my body morphs into something I hate...

A slight change here and there,

Never staying the way it should.

I don't get other people,

Don't they see how hideous I look?

Why do they always approach me?

Why do they say I'm fine?

I'm clearly not fine.

I avoid mirrors wherever I go,

They are a portal to my own hell.

Every detail stands out to me,

Everything seems so glaringly obvious.

No amount of surgical morphing will ever help me,

No amount of makeup will make me feel like me...

I'm a walking freak show,

I try to hide what others can't see.

I just wish I could see who I'm meant to be.

ANDROPHOBIA

I'm afraid of men,

Plain and simple,

Just the thought of them makes me shiver.

Even when I know I'm not in danger I can't help but shake in fear
as I walk past them...

I never truly had a father figure,

I was alone since birth,

Raised from a single mother.

I'm a man,

Or at least I'm a boy,

I don't understand,

I'm scared of the very gender I am...

If I try to talk about it I get called a sissy,

Grow up! Stop being a child!

I'm sorry, I can't help it...

I shut off my doors,

If a man gets near I run,

I run as far away as I can because I am afraid…

I'm afraid of what's to come.

My father was an alcoholic,

A vile creature that crept around at night,

He still lives inside my head,

He is the monster under my bed.

I know everyone isn't the same...

I know not everyone is out to hurt me.

I'm sorry if I can't help but steer away from the gender that makes
me recall danger.

PSYCHOPATH

I was born this way,

I was born to lead,

I was born for greatness..

What's wrong with lying?

Nothing.

I get my way,

And everyones fine.

I'm an unemotional corpse,

I'm a zombie in the living world,

Sadness? What's that?

It's not in my vocabulary.

I was born with the inability to determine right or wrong,

The inability to understand or comprehend emotions.

My IQ is something you can't comprehend,

With the power of my words I can make you do my bidding.

I play everyone like a toy,

I'm not who you believe I am,

I'm not who people perceive me to be.

Look deeper,

Through the crooks and crannies of my brain,

Look deeper,

You will find a stone cold heart,

Look deeper,

If you ever dare.